Saving
THE
WIFE!
THIS IS KEY!

Saving THE WIFE! THIS IS KEY!

To Keep the Vow "For Better or For WORST"
When the worst has happened

Tiffany T. Helms

XULON PRESS

Xulon Press
555 Winderley Pl, Suite 225
Maitland, FL 32751
407.339.4217
www.xulonpress.com

Paperback ISBN-13: 978-1-66289-096-3
eBook ISBN-13: 978-1-66289-097-0

Acknowledgements

"Oh' taste and see the goodness of the Lord!" (Psalm 34:8) If it had not been for the Lord on my side, this book would not have made it to fruition. I would like to thank my Lord and Savior, Jesus Christ, for holding my hand through the journey, for keeping me, for the test, for the trial, and for the triumph. There were many times that I questioned God about this assignment, and *His* answer was still *"Yes."* There were many times that I was distracted from this purpose, but the Lord never left me. The Lord made a way to grab my attention over and over again. I am so grateful for the *Holy Spirit* being my best teacher, my corrector, and my defense. I would like to thank my supportive husband for his willingness to allow me to share some of his story through my story. I would like to thank my beautiful mother, Viola and Lee (a life saver) for being a big help to my children and me during my test and trial. I especially wish to thank every single person that motivated me, that uplifted me, that gave me truth in the face of fear, and that reminded me of this purposed assignment.

Table of Contents

Intro

(Thee Wife)

"How do you save the Wife?" is the question you may be asking in your head. This is Key! To actually be saved is to give your life to Jesus Christ.

Wife! Are you saved?

Saving the Wife is about being saved by Christ Jesus first and foremost. More importantly, it is about being saved from divorce when the worst of life's trials have happened in your marriage. The title "Saving the Wife" comes from the need to be saved from making bad decisions as the Wife, who is the rib and also the helpmate to the husband when going through the rough. This book is to prevent you from sinning in your marriage due to negative circumstances. Moreover, it is to deter you from getting even with your husband when he has done you wrong.

    Saving the Wife is simply about saving yourself, saving your identity as the wife, and saving the most cherished, precious, and powerful thing that the Most High God blessed you with—***Your Marriage!*** Most notably, *Saving the Wife* is about keeping the vow, "For better or for *worst*," when the worst is happening or has happened. This book is to uplift you, the Wife, and witness to you from experience—the experience of how I was empowered even in the rough and tough of my marriage. Key factors to live by as a wife while going through tough times are highlighted in this book. My prayer is that you find hope for your marriage if you have lost hope. I pray that you gain faith in God for your marriage, even if you just can't believe in your husband anymore.

It is my prayer that this book helps you to remember and embrace the significance of your marriage. I pray that you are ministered to through biblical scripture that is used. If you are not saved in the midst of your own sins, I pray that as you read, you are compelled to give your life to Christ. My ultimate prayer is that you are encouraged to endure through the worst with your husband when situations seem too hard to bear. I declare and decree, in Jesus's name, favor for your marriage to blossom from the seeds of love, faith, forgiveness, and repentance that are planted in this book. Victory is yours! By the blood of Jesus, sweat and tears, Wife, we shall stand! Troubles do not last always. Be the Wife! You are the Wife! Stand your ground!

Chapter 1

Covenant (The Promise)

So, your dream came true. Hallelujah to God! You have him! You have the man that you just could not sleep without. The man you just could not contain yourself from. The man you think or thought was all that and a snicker with nuts. The wedding day happened. Oh, and you had on the dress. The wedding was your favorite colors too. Oh, how beautiful! Whether you went to the courthouse or had a big extravagant wedding, you married the man that tickles your fancy, the man that makes you feel good on the inside, the man that you are so proud to say, "That's my husband!" Yaaaaassss! *Your Husband!* Remember that! You married the man that is now your earthly king!

Wife, do you remember becoming the *Mrs.?* Do you recall becoming the one and only top priority of his? Wife, do you remember signing your signature on those papers? This is Key! Those papers are not just words in black and white. Those papers hold weight, legally. Those papers hold life, spiritually.

Those marriage papers are the proof of a promise, a commitment, an agreement to be with each other in this life, doing life together, enjoying each other, loving each other, learning each other more and more, sacrificing for each other, wining and dining each other, and even standing and staying with each other during the worst of times.

When you said, "I do," did you think of anything else other than that moment? Nope! I bet you didn't even think about what was next. I know I didn't. I was so overwhelmed with happiness that I ended up taking pictures without refreshing my lip gloss. Now, you know that's a no-no! You just made a promise before the Most High God in the church or before the judge in the courthouse or at a pretty nice venue in front of the minister … huh! Either way, you made that promise not knowing what the future would hold. Of course, hopes and dreams and goals and wishes had been talked about way before the wedding day. I know! But the only thing that we knew for sure is that we were marrying the most handsome man and moving forward, making it official. For some, you were officially not sinning anymore if you were fornicating. For others, you were officially about to make-out for real, if you were waiting, and most officially, you were now "Thee Wife" if you were already performing wifely duties. As for me, I had seen a dream come true right before my eyes by marrying my favorite friend of three years, whom I risked my salvation and soul for. I was officially done shacking and officially done grooving and "smooving" without the Lord approving! For all, we were officially his beneficiary!

Therefore shall a man leave his father and his mother,
and shall cleave unto his wife: and they shall be one flesh.
Genesis 2:24 (KJV)

Now, This is Key! What did you say "I do" to? Did the minister ask you, "Do you take this man to be your husband, to have and to hold, **till death** do you part?" I know you said, "I do!" Are you dead yet? You? Not trust! You? Not communication! You? Not romance! You? Not finances! You? Not understanding! You? Are **YOU** dead? If you are not dead, then your marriage is not dead. You and your husband are *one* flesh. If your husband is still alive, then your marriage is yet alive. It may not be thriving the way that it should be because of lack. However, Wife, when you are a woman of virtue, you are above lack because of your strength. You should have the strength in knowing that where there is lack, there also is the Lord to fill the gap. Your husband knows that you are a virtuous woman. That is why he married you. He could trust you with his heart. Please believe that his heart is still beating for you, even in the midst of a storm.

In a marriage, things may not go as we think they should (or even know they should) go. As a wife, we have to keep our promises even when the trust is gone, even when communication is lacking, even when the romance is dry, even when the finances are low, even when we just do not understand what is going on. **The Bible tells us that a virtuous woman "will do her husband good and not evil for all the days of her life" (Proverbs 31:12 KJV).** It will not be good to renege on your promise of "till death do you part." Wife, are you a woman of your word? This may seem harsh when the worst has happened in your marriage, and it is if you do not know or have a relationship with the Man that sits high and looks low—a relationship with the Creator of Heaven and Earth, the Author and Finisher of Faith, the Great I Am, the Prince of Peace, our Lord and Savior, Jesus. It is imperative that Jesus be a part of our marriage.

"Jesus is the way, the truth and the life," declares the Holy Bible (John 14:6 KJV).

Therefore, Jesus is the Judge of the marriage. Why else would we go to the church to get married or have a minister to marry us or even have a judge in the courthouse to marry us? Wife, we need that higher power to keep us, to help us, and to guide our marriage with truth. We made a covenant not only with our husband; it was also made with the Most High God. If it were not so, we could have just said, "I do," in the bedroom and ran with that instead of having a man or woman of the cloth of God to marry us. What exactly is a covenant? You ask. A **covenant** rests on the concept of a power higher than man which gives proper authority to carry out any particular end that the **covenant** is seeking to reach. So, This is Key; you and your husband are covenant partners seeking to conquer a successful marriage. **The Bible tells us in Romans 8:37 (KJV) that "we are more than conquerors" through Jesus.** So, in order to live up to your promise, Wife, you have to rely on

God, the highest power. However, the only way you are going to get to God is through Jesus. Life happens, and we need our husband. The Holy Bible says in **Ecclesiastes 4:9-12 (KJV)**:

> *Two are better than one; because they have a good reward for their labour. For if they fall, the one will lift up his fellow: but woe to him that is alone when he falleth; for he hath not another to help him up. Again, if two lie together, then they have heat: but how can one be warm alone? And if one prevail against him, two shall withstand him; and a threefold cord is not quickly broken.*

Amen! A threefold cord is you, the Most High God, and your husband! See, This is Key! God in the center of your marriage will keep your marriage and remind you of the promises that you vowed before *Him.*

Wife! The covenant, the promise, the commitment, and the vows are all an authentication of love. What is love? The Holy Bible tells us in **1 Corinthians 13:4-8 (NIV)**, *"Love is patient, love is kind. It does not envy, it does not boast, it is not proud. It does not dishonor others, it is not self-seeking, it is not easily angered, it keeps no record of wrongs. Love does not delight in evil but rejoices with the truth. It always protects, always trusts, always hopes, always perseveres. Love never fails!"* **Amen!** Do you love your husband? The question is not asking, "Are you *in love* with your husband?" As I have come to realize, those may be two different aspects of loving. We make the decision to love continually after we have fallen in love. What about when we fall out of love? I am sure that in a marriage, you won't feel butterflies every year because of life's quarrels. So, when those butterflies fall asleep, we still have to love. As a wife, to love should be our first decision. What does it mean to love?

It means to...

Learn each other and from each other by listening, observing, and putting toward actions that coincide with what we have grown to know.

It means to...

Organize spending time together, creating heartfelt moments.

To love means to...

Value each other! To value not only the body but the soul, the opinions, the time, and the efforts of one another. When we value our husband, we will take care of him in every way possible.

It means to...

Excite the mind. Excitement releases endorphins in our spirit that bring about happiness and creates an atmosphere conducive to the success of our marriage.

I'm sure some people married for different reasons. Some people say they married for finances (cause he buy me this and that, and red bottoms), for companionship (just don't want to be alone), for looks (oh, he's too fine), or to simply have help in the house (sharing bills). However, the main reason to marry is for love.

Love hides a multitude of faults, which helps to keep our promises if or when the worst part happens. The Bible proclaims in **1 Peter 4:8 (NIV),** *"Above all, love each other deeply, because love covers over a multitude of sins."* **Amen!** And boy oh boy, do we need love to cover for us. (Chapter 4 will discuss this further.) I am glad I married for love. I also married my husband because the Bible says, *"It is better to marry than to burn if you just can't contain yourself"* **(1 Corinthians 7:9 KJV).** And baby, I could not contain myself. Furthermore, I married him because he asked! He got down on one knee, right by the trash can in our kitchen, in the middle of me cooking breakfast; he kneeled right in front of me (so sweet) and told me that he could not live without me. I am sure that your husband did pretty much the same thing and much more romantically, which shows right there that he chose you and cannot live this life without you. You are his good thing!

He that findeth a wife, findeth a good thing, and obtains Favor from the Lord. **Proverbs 18:22 (KJV)**

Wife, *please believe,* our marriage is our shelter. It keeps us in the blessed place. We are blessed to be ourselves and not hide our flaws—blessed in our passions and blessed in our hopes and in our dreams. Our marriage saves us from sin against our own body. We have a covenant partner, someone to touch and agree with in the *mighty* name of Jesus, whom is our very own individual husband. Wife, we are favored! Let us keep our covenant sacred, in spite of disaster. The sacred marriage is the one that lasts.

Question? This is Key!

Why did you get married? List Five Reasons ...

1.

2.

3.

4.

5.

What do you actually like about your husband? His character? Handsomeness? Strength? His generosity? What?

Focus on those attributes of your marriage and your husband and give the rest to the Most High God in prayer, believing that the Lord will take care of every shortcoming, every downfall, every trial, and every situation and circumstance at hand. Amen!

We are in this to win this! When we focus on the positives, there is no way that the negative forces will overtake us and have us thinking about the "Big D" ...

DIVORCE.

Divorce is the most negative solution to any hard trial in a marriage.

The Bible declares in Malachi 2:16 (NKJV) that "'the LORD God of Israel HATES divorce, For it covers one's garment with violence,' says the LORD of hosts. 'Therefore take heed to your spirit that you do not deal treacherously.'" Amen!

See, This is Key! Divorce is not an option. It is definitely not a part of the promise. We have to adopt that mindset about our marriage. Knowing now that God hates divorce, there should never come a time where a wife speaks it out of her mouth. Divorce is not love. Divorce is totally against God's plan for us. As a matter of fact, divorce is the devil's mechanism to steal, kill, and destroy. The devil wants to destroy your marriage and steal your joy and kill your faith in God. Anything that the Lord has promised us and has made for us to prosper in life, that treacherous devil wants to snatch it away from us without a fight. So, we, as the Wife, cannot let Satan rule in our life by taking control of our mindset and turning it against the union of God. It is just like this: Would you let someone snatch something out of your hand without trying to snatch it back or putting up a fight to get it back? I don't think so!

> **The Bible says in 1 Corinthians 7:10-11 (NKJV),** **"Now to the married I command,** *yet* not I but the Lord: A wife is not to depart from *her* husband. **But even if she does depart, let her remain unmarried or be reconciled to** *her* husband. And a husband is not to divorce *his* wife."

Our marriage is so significant to God. Divorce demolishes the entire concept of the covenant. The Lord's design for marriage is for us to be fruitful and multiply, and not just fruitful in producing children. The Lord wants us to be fruitful in every area of our life with our husband. God's desire is for us to be fruitful in our faith, fruitful in our finances, fruitful in intimacy, fruitful in our purpose, and fruitful in our relationship with Him. If we are going to be fruitful, our mindset on our marriage cannot be in a graven state. Our mindset should be in a growth state. Just because dirt has piled up on your marriage does not mean it is dead and buried. You have to look at it differently. You have to think, if trials come to make you stronger, then your marriage is not buried but planted for growth. I know when my husband and I had our first real trial in our marriage; I thought it was the end of the world. My mind was so messed up because I could not believe that something so bad was happening in my marriage because of my husband's own individual fault. Of course, I thought about divorce. That was an ungodly mindset! After praying and praying about it, I then thought about the vow "For better or for *worst*," and my mind was stuck on that promise. Then, I began to seek God more to help me keep my promise and actually mean "for better or for worst" in my heart. See, I did not want to deal with the worst part. I felt some things should never happen in a marriage. In reality, some things will happen in our marriage, and our mindset should already know "no matter what comes or what goes," it is for better or for worst. Then we can begin to grow instead of being stuck in the problem and not seeking a better solution.

This is Key! You have to still want to be a Wife. The good Wife! His good thing!

Question:

What do you love about being a Wife to your husband?

Wife! What do your marriage vows mean to you?

Now, how do you *really* keep the vow, "For better or for worse"? More easily said than done, right? Especially when the husband is acting up with disrespect, unfaithfulness, irresponsibility, alcoholism, and drug addiction that makes it hard to forgive him and trust him. Well, first, it starts with you— the God in you!

Chapter 2

Savior (The God in You)

Therefore if any man be in Christ, he is a new creature: old things are passed away; behold, all things are become new.
2 Corinthians 5:17 (KJV)

This is Key! In order for God to be in you, you have to be in Christ, our Lord and Savior, Jesus. This is important because when you are in Christ, you adopt a new spirit—the Spirit of our Savior. Having our Savior's Spirit inside of you helps you to sustain a position of a loving, caring, and nurturing Wife in spite of hardship. It is the fruit of the Spirit that we need in order to overcome difficulty. What is the fruit of the Spirit? You ask.

Love, Joy, Peace, Longsuffering, Kindness, Goodness, Faithfulness, Gentleness, Self-control.

Galatians 5:22-23 (NKJV)

So, definitely, we need the Holy Spirit of God if we want to have joy and peace in the midst of a storm! God's Spirit is free! We just have to grab it and hold on to it. Your life depends on *His* Spirit. The Spirit of God places us in a blessed state of mind, no matter what the circumstance is. If you don't have the fruit of the Spirit right now, let's go to the drawing board and get it. The drawing board starts with a prayer of repentance. Declare this prayer in your heart:

Father God, in the mighty name of Jesus,

Thank you so much for loving me, thank you so much for Your loving kindness and tender mercy on my life. Lord, Your grace is sufficient for me, and I thank you. Heavenly Father, I come in need of a Savior. I ask that You forgive me for my sins, forgive me for anything that I have done wrong, said wrong, thought wrong, for anything that was not pleasing to Your will and to Your way. Lord, I ask that You create a clean heart within me and renew my mind so that I may be more like You. Lord, I ask that You search me O'God, and if You find anything that is not like You, pluck it out, Jesus. I relinquish all of the hurt, pain, disappointment, fear, and worry to You, O'God. I give You my heart, Jesus, and I give You my mind, Lord. Lord, I'm standing in the need of a blessing. You are everything that I need to endure, to push, to keep going in my marriage. Lord, You purposed marriage for Your glory. I give my marriage to You in the condition that it is in right now.

Lord, You make all things new, and I am leaning on You for restoration. I bind the enemy hand in my marriage. I ask in Jesus's name that You destroy the yolk, O'God. Destroy the yolk of bondage, the yolk of un-equalness. I plead the blood of Jesus over my life, over my husband's life, and over my marriage. Father God, I stretch my hand to Thee, for You are the God of all. You are a burden bearer, heavy-load lifter, a mind regulator, and a peace stimulator. I bless Your name, Jesus, and I welcome Your Holy Spirit in my heart and in my life. Thank you for the washing, for the purging, for the blood of Jesus. Lord, thank you for Your fruit of the Spirit. I declare and decree a Spirit-filled life. Dwell within me so that I may carry out my duties as a wife, the wife You envisioned in Your image. O'God, thank you for Jesus, thank you for being a savior, Thank you for the cross. God, thank you for Christ redeemed. I believe in You, Jesus. I believe You died and arose from the dead in three days with all power in Your hands. I love You, and I praise Your name, for it is great and greatly to be praised. Lord, I lift Your name on high, and I turn from my wicked ways. Lord, God, I give You permission to change me for the better, to change me for Your glory, and to change my walk and my talk. Lord, I declare and decree a healthy lifestyle with the desire to please You in Jesus's name. Thank you! Thank you! Thank you! All of this I ask in Jesus's mighty name. I pray, Amen!

YES, AND IT IS SO!

Just like that, we are in God, and God is in us. All we have to do now is embrace Jesus. We have to embrace everything we know about the Lord. The primary thing we know is that Jesus is a Holy Spirit that dwells in our heart. The first fruit of God's Holy Spirit is *love*, which holds no conditions. That kind of love is now resting upon our bosom. The love that our Father God gives us is unconditional. No matter what we do, Jesus loves us still. If we cuss like a sailor, Jesus loves us still. If we get drunk and start acting crazy, Jesus loves us still. If we commit a crime, guess what? Jesus loves us still, unconditionally. Jesus's love will still reign on us even in our sin because His love holds no conditions.

This is Key! The unconditional love that our Father God gives to us, we, the Wife, have to give the same unconditional love to our husband. We have to see our husband as a human being wrapped in flesh and covered in the blood of Jesus, just as God sees us. Therefore, conditions should never be attached to love. Unconditional love sometimes takes time to flourish in our mind as we are conditioned to love a man by the way the man treats us. For that reason, when we begin to feel as if we are being treated poorly and inconsiderably, the condition of love changes, and our mindset for our mate changes too. I had to grow into the place of unconditional love for my husband. At first, my love for him was all about conditions. It was, "If he doesn't stop this, if he don't do that, and if he can't, then I'm not about to stick around for him to do whatever he wants to do." I needed him to do what I said in regard to his own life. Wow! That was the wrong way to treat my husband. At that time, I felt it was the right way since the conditions changed from him being all about me to him being all about the streets. Wife, what we say to our husband is about 98 percent right all the time. Right? Get this though! This is Key! Our husbands are individuals with their own mind, their own desires, their own ambitions, their own outlook on life, and with their own cross to bear. They are entitled to make their own mistakes without thinking that we, the wife, are going to leave them. When husbands feel that their mistakes will cause the marriage to end, they start to keep secrets. Wife, we do not want our husband to keep any secrets from us. This is why it is so important to show love unconditionally. Our husband need to feel accepted and not rejected based off of conditions that may surface one day. I first embraced unconditional love for my husband when I came to a point in my mind that questioned, "What matters *most* to me?" I answered that question too. The answer was not that he catered to my every wish and command; the answer was not that he stopped running the streets, although it mattered. The answer that mattered the most to me was that he came home safe at night and that we spend this life together, loving, regardless of the misunderstandings, mishaps, tests, and trials. This is not saying that the husband can be out cheating as long as he comes home at night. This is not that! Wife, it is ultimately a decision to love unconditionally over and over again.

"For God so loved the world, that he gave his only begotten Son, that whosoever believeth in him should not perish, but have everlasting life."
John 3:16 (KJV)

God made the decision to love us so beyond measure. Our Father God showed His love by sacrificing and giving up His only Son for our sins. This sounds like God made a big decision, a life changing decision. Right! Now, we also know that love sacrifices and gives the first, the last, and the only. Sometimes, as the Wife, we will have to sacrifice something to show our husband real love, Godly love, and fruit of the Spirit love.

The second fruit of the spirit is *joy*. How do we have joy when we feel unhappy with our husband because of his unchanged behavior? This is Key! **"The Joy of the Lord is your strength"** (**Nehemiah 8:10 KJV**). I know you may be thinking about what strength has to do with the happiness that the joy of the Lord gives. Well, strength is all about the ability to overcome unhappiness when God's unspeakable joy overtakes your heart. We get joy by seeking God and thanking God right in the midst of a situation that's out of our hands. Joy is found in the knowledge of knowing that God is in control and His mercy endures forever. So, whatever the situation is with your husband, have joy in knowing that God is a way maker, a provider, a protector, a mind regulator, a burden barrier, and heavy-load sharer. It is not enough in just knowing though. We have to open up our mouth and give God praises for it. We have to make joyful noises by singing hymns and spirituals. That is when the real joy rests upon our heart and turns our mean-mug to a Kool-Aid smile.

Peace is the third fruit of the Spirit. If we don't have peace in our mind, we are easily frustrated, easily angered, and easily stressed out. This is why peace in our spirit is so important to have. How do we have peace in our spirit when things are chaotic? This is Key! The scripture Philippians 4:6-9 (KJV) tells us:

> *Be careful for nothing; but in every thing by prayer and supplication with thanksgiving, let your requests be made known unto God.*

> *And the PEACE of God, which passeth all understanding, shall keep your hearts and minds through Christ Jesus.*

> *Finally, brethren, whatsoever things are true, whatsoever things are honest, whatsoever things are just, whatsoever things are pure, whatsoever things are lovely, whatsoever things are of good report; if there be any virtue, and if there be any praise, think on these things.*

> *Those things, which ye have both learned, and received, and heard, and seen in me, do: and the God of PEACE shall be with you.*

> *AMEN!*

*In other words, peace is found in prayer, praise, and pondering on the positives **daily.***

Longsuffering is one of the fruits of the Spirit that a Wife should definitely possess. We do not know what our marriage will face or how long we will have to endure in a situation. Having longsuffering in our spirit will determine our fight or flight response. We will automatically fight for our marriage if we have longsuffering dwelling in our heart. Contrary, when we don't have longsuffering abiding in our heart, flight will be the natural instinct when troubles come. When we are fleshly, without the fruit of the Spirit, it is much easier to act on leaving a situation and leaving the marriage due to mishaps.

Having patience is sometimes considered as having long-suffering; however, patience is very different from longsuffering. Patience does not require you to fight. On the other hand, longsuffering does. Fighting is required in longsuffering because we really don't want to suffer long. So, in order to get pass the feeling of longsuffering, we have to fight back. What does it mean to fight back? Well, it is like this: If a flying bug flew toward your face, automatically, you are going to start swinging until the bug has flown elsewhere. The same with marriage; some stuff just flies in that we want to fly out just as quick as it flew in. So, the fight we put up is for it to stop, for it to go, for it to be over … whatever "it" is. This is Key. We do our fighting in prayer! In longsuffering, we have to P.U.S.H.! Pray Until Something Happens!

Kindness and *Goodness* are two more fruits of the Spirit that we, the Wife, really need to possess as characteristics of ourselves anyway. Have you ever met a rude and nasty person, and their attitude just stinks? Well, it is not good for a wife to have a stinky attitude toward her husband. Cause guess what? There are women out in the streets that are nice, talk slick, and smile. We don't need to create any problems from the lack of kindness and goodness toward our husband. I know that when it is tough, we really don't want to be bothered. We just want to see a change. Get this—Be the change! This is Key. God has given us a spirit of kindness and goodness; use it to your advantage. When we are kind in negative circumstances, it confuses the Enemy, and it changes the atmosphere. If you operate in the flesh, you will be tempted to have a bad attitude and a stinky demeanor toward your husband during hard times. This is why it is so important to *seek* God. The Bible says in Matthew 6:33 (KJV), **"Seek ye first the Kingdom of God, and his righteousness; and all these things shall be added unto you."** A Godly heart will be added unto you which produces kindness and goodness as a result of being filled with a fruitful spirit.

Faithfulness is the seventh fruit of the Spirit. We all know what the number seven represents. Winning! In the spiritual realm, it means "completion." So, in order to be winning and complete in your walk with the Most High God, you have to be loyal to God. Loyalty is Key! **"The Lord is close to the brokenhearted and He saves those who are crushed in spirit"**

21

(Psalm 34:18 NIV). So, the Lord is not only close to us when things are going perfectly fine; He is especially close to us when things are heart wrenching, devastating, and dreadful. The Lord is so faithful. From that, we know that the Lord will never leave us nor forsake us. We have to have that same faithfulness to *Him* in our fellowship with believers, in our worship, in our praise, in our prayer life, and even through witnessing the goodness of God. Faithfulness is a standard and a requirement of being in God and of God being in you. Period!

I know that, when things are out of control in marriage and situations seem too hard to bear, we tend to question where God is. God is saying, "I am right where you left Me. Come back, pick Me up, and place Me in your heart." Then we question, "Why would God let this happen?" We may also question if there really is a God. I questioned that one day! Then I looked at my handsome young children that the Lord blessed me with when everybody counted me out of motherhood. Instantly, I remembered that the Lord counted me in, in His timing. Praise God! So, God is up there, and God is up to something big in our marriage in His timing. We should be faithful to God, which will automatically make us faithful to our husband, regardless of the condition or state our marriage is in.

Faithfulness also includes having faith. **The Bible declares that without faith, it is impossible to please God (Hebrews 11:6 NIV).** We, as the Wife, should want to please God. So, let us embrace faith, the substance of things hoped for, the evidence of things not seen. How do we embrace faith in hard times? First, we have to have hope. We have to hope that the Lord will bring us out of the storm without the storm overtaking our marriage. Then once we have hope, we have to keep hope alive. Then that hope turns into faith. I am reminded of the biblical story where Jesus was on the boat asleep. *His* disciples, who were on the same boat, were scared that the windstorm would destroy them. The disciples went and woke Jesus up and asked *Him* if *He* even cared if they died because of the storm raging so badly. I know sometimes, we may feel like God doesn't care about our situation when the storm is raging. The Bible says that Jesus got up and rebuked the wind and said peace be still. Instantly, the storm was over, and all Jesus wanted to know was why did they not have faith. (*Mark 4:37-40*). Wife, we ought to be able to activate our faith when faced with adversity because God is on the boat. Wake *Him* up and cast your cares on *Him*. Once we give our cares to *Him*, we should walk with the faith in knowing that, when God speaks to situations, they cease. Then we are on our journey of faithfulness.

I remember when I was about ten years old, and I lost my quarter in my bedroom. I looked all over my bedroom for that quarter. I looked on the bed, under the bed, on the dresser, behind the dresser, in the windowpane, and all over the floor, and I could not find it anywhere. I wanted that quarter so bad. I dropped to my knees and started praying to God, hoping that He would hear me and help me find my quarter. I got up off my knees ready to see this quarter that I asked God about. Guess what? My quarter was sitting right on top of the fan in my room. Wow! I could have sworn that I'd looked on top of that fan before I prayed. One would say that the quarter was there all along. Another would say that God is not magical enough to make a quarter appear when it wasn't there. This is why we need God. The Lord helps us to see things clearly and put things back in place in our lives.

Ultimately, This is Key! *Childlike faith!* We have to have childlike faith—the kind of faith that *believes* everything about God and about our situation—that it is going to get better. You know kids believe everything they hear, and they expect everything to be given to them. So, just as a child believes what is said about God, that He can do all things, we should believe in every word of God also. **The Bible declares that faith cometh by hearing, and hearing by the word of God (Romans 10:17 KJV).** All we need is a pinch of hope, and that will create a mustard seed of faith. A mustard seed of faith can move mountains. I would like to add that our faith should always be in the Most High God and not in man. You should not have faith in man for a change, for a blessing, or for an outcome. It is so easy to lose sight of faith when faced with trials and tribulations, especially when your faith is in your husband. Having faith in God above your husband takes the pressure off of man, who can fail, and puts the pressure on God, who cannot fail. Wow! It may seem ideal to seek answers outside of God when our focus is not on God. However, This is Key! Only God can do the impossible or make a difficulty easy. So, *faith it until God manifests it!* Amen!

Speaking of manifestation, the Holy Bible declares that faith without works is dead (James 2:20 KJV). Wife, we have to put the work in to embrace our faith in God. Embracing our faith means that we not only believe in God, but we are standing on every word of God by working for God. What qualifies as "works in faith"?

This is Key! **C.O.P.D.**

    C- *Confidence* in the Lord, knowing that He is able to do extraordinarily in abundance of all that we ask or think (Ephesians 3:20).

    O- *Obedience* in following the commandments of God and becoming more Christ-like.

    P- *Preparation is Key!* Prepare for what is to come by using your confidence in God to move you and your actions toward the expected outcome.

    D- *Discipline* your mind to think positively, Discipline your tongue to speak life into the situation. Discipline your response when faced with negativity.

Gentleness is the eighth fruit of the Spirit. It is imperative that a wife displays gentleness to her husband. Gentleness is the outcome of operating in humility. A wife is gentler when pride is set to the side. Gentleness comes from knowing that we all fall short of the glory of God. When we operate from a non-judgmental place, we can respond gently when faced with problems in our marriage that were caused by our husband. Being gentle means being soft spoken and using your words wisely when speaking. Using your words wisely means that you are choosing words that are not mean and degrading to your husband. You are choosing words that speak life and love in a situation. Your words should put your husband at ease and help him to release his feelings in a gentle way to you. Speaking to your husband with a mean demeanor and tone creates an atmosphere of chaos and negativity. When there is chaos and negativity in the air, arguments tend to get out of control. So, it is best to talk to your husband in a way that shows care, concern, gentleness, and respect. **"A gentle answer turns away wrath, but a harsh word stirs up anger" (Proverbs 15:1 NIV).**

We have come to the last, but definitely not measured least, fruit of the Spirit, which is *self-control.* I cannot express enough how important it is to have self-control in our marriage, including self-control in our everyday walk with Christ. Self-control is by far the most valuable quality of a Wife. *This is Key! We need self-control when we have a desire to please ourselves in the midst of a storm instead of a desire to please the Lord.* When marriage seems hard and we really want to quit, having self-control will keep us from the actions of quitting. What are the actions of quitting in a marriage? You ask. Quitting in marriage is taking off your wedding ring. Ooh! Please, do not do that! The devil is watching and will see that ring finger missing the ring. When the devil sees that, there goes a spark of a conversation from a cheating man that thinks he has got a chance because of the light discoloration on your wedding ring finger. An unsaved wife would probably think, "What better time than this to gain attention from a man," when not getting any attention at home. So, no; we do not want to create a situation that will lead to an affair. Quitting in marriage is entertaining another man in secret, going out clubbing to seek a friend, acting like you don't care when you really do, making your husband cook for himself when you are the one who always cooks, staying out late at night, not calling your husband throughout the day, refusing to iron his clothes when you normally do, and withholding intimacy. Withholding Intimacy is a big deal. I remember when my husband and I were going through a rough patch. He wanted to make love, but I did not. I was totally disgusted with him because of the way he was choosing to live his life. My husband had started hanging out with the wrong crowd, getting high by popping pills, drinking syrup, and being very irresponsible. He was not the man I married. His character diminished from being an honest, respectable, responsible, providing man to such a failure in my eyes. I was totally out of patience with him. I did not even trust him anymore. So, no, I did not want to be intimate with him. He blew up at me, saying that I am his wife, and a wife is supposed to please her husband. He was right! The Bible says in **1 Corinthians 7:3-5 (NKJV)**, *"Let the husband render to his wife the affection due to her, and likewise also the wife to her husband. The wife does not have authority over her own body, but the husband does.* **And likewise the husband does not have authority over his**

own body, but the wife *does*." I felt so horrible. He wanted to be pleasured so bad that night. I gave in to his needs. The whole time, I literally cried. I was crying because I did not have any intimate desires for him anymore. I was devastatingly heartbroken. Those tears were tears of anger, frustration, and simply, pain. Nevertheless, He seemed to enjoy it. After we were done, I rushed to the restroom crying my heart out, sitting on the toilet to make sure that all of his body fluids left my body. I could not imagine being impregnated by my husband that night, even though I wanted a baby so desperately. I am sharing this with you because something significant happened that night. From that physical interlude that I did not want to be a part of, our very first child was conceived. Wow! My husband and I had been trying to have a baby for seven years. Look at God in the midst of disappointment, in the midst of a trial. Had I not done it, my baby probably would not even be here today. So, withholding intimacy is not the key. Intimacy was made for husband and wife. It was made to aid in reconciliation of marriage, among other things. How can we expect our husband to be faithful when we are withholding sex? Think about it! The Bible even tells us in **1 Corinthians 7:5 (NKJV), "Do not deprive one another except with consent for a time, that you may give yourselves to fasting and prayer; and come together again so that Satan does not tempt you because of your lack of self-control."**

So, before we can control our actions, we must control our thoughts.

This is Key! Cast down every imagination and desire that does not align itself with being a good wife. It doesn't matter if your husband is not being a good husband right now. Marriage is not about tit for tat ("You be good, I'll be good," "You be bad, I'll be bad.") No! As a wife, we have a standard to uphold. Wife, we are queens! We don't do certain things, and that is why we need self-control. Self-control is about holding our tongue when we really want to curse our husband out. Self-control is about not going through our husband's phone seeking to find something against him. Self-control is also about keeping our marital problems within the sanctity of our marriage with God and not seeking ungodly counsel from friends and family.

2 Peter 1:5-8 (NIV) tells us:

For this very reason, make every effort to add to your faith, goodness; and to goodness, knowledge; and to knowledge, self-control; and to self-control, perseverance; and to perseverance, godliness; and to godliness, mutual affection; and to mutual affection, love. For if you possess these qualities in increasing measure, they will keep you from being ineffective and unproductive in your knowledge of our Lord Jesus Christ.

So, in order to be effective in self-control, we have to adopt the mindset of Christ. Amen!

Wife, we need the mindset of the Lord and not the mind of the world for marriage. The world will tell us to leave our husband if he is acting up, if he loses his job, if he fall victim to drugs, or if he go to jail. The world will also tell us to cheat back if we find out our husband is cheating. **So, "Be not conformed to this world, but be ye transformed by the renewing of your mind that ye may prove what is that good, and acceptable, and perfect, will of God." Amen! (Romans 12:2 KJV)**

How do we renew our mind?

> **By casting down imaginations, and every high thing that exalteth itself against the knowledge of God, and bringing into captivity every thought to the obedience of Christ. (2 Corinthians 10:5 KJV)**

What does God tell us in the face of adversity?

> **Put on the whole armour of God that ye may be able to stand against the wiles of the devil. For we wrestle not against flesh and blood, but against principalities, against powers, against the rulers of the darkness of this world, against spiritual wickedness in high places. Wherefore take unto you the whole armour of God, that ye may be able to withstand in the evil day, and having done all, to stand. (Ephesians 6:11-13 KJV)**

Well, what is the whole armour of God? You ask.

The whole armour of God includes *the helmet of salvation,* which frees us from bondage, sin, and guiltiness; *the breastplate of righteousness* gives us the ability to walk upright and speak and do what thus says the Lord. *The belt of truth* allows us to be victorious in the name of Jesus. *The sword of the spirit* gives us power and authority against our enemies. *The shield of faith* makes the impossible possible. *Our feet are protected by the gospel of the Lord,* which provides direction of our steps and aligns them in order (Ephesians 6:14-18). Yes, we need all of that to *stand* against the devil's tactics to destroy us, our husband, our marriage, and to survive the worst.

This is Key! We have to know without a shadow of doubt that it is the Enemy's attack on our marriage and on our husband.

It is true that the Enemy, the devil, the ruler of the darkness of this world, attacks anything that God has positioned together to stop God's purpose and God's plan. It is our duty as a Wife to stand in the gap for our husband and our marriage when under the torch. Standing in the gap means being an intercessor by praying, fasting, praising, and waging war. I am reminded of a story in the Bible from the Book of Esther. Esther, the queen, fasted and prayed for three days in hopes to find favor from King Ahasuerus. Queen Esther went to the king after those three days, petitioning that he grant life to her people, the Jews, and specifically Mordecai, as there was a hit out on him and the Jews. Queen Esther fell to the king's feet, crying and pleading for him to stop the evil that was planned against the Jews and Mordecai. The king found her pleasing to his eyes and granted her request! Hallelujah to God! Wife, the same thing goes for us. We have to make ourselves pleasing to God's sight when we want the Lord, *King Jesus*, to move on our behalf. We have to purposefully *seek* God's face when the devil is attacking our home. Only the God within us will help us to see that the devil is working overtime to destroy our happiness, our marriage, and our faith in God. If we think that it is just our husband that is acting up, think again. Bad spirits attach themselves to people, and those same bad spirits will attach themselves to us. Then we will find ourselves trying to get back at our husband for something he did to us. That is so devilish. We want to steer clear of a devilish mind by constantly renewing our mind, standing on the word of God for our marriage, and being obedient to God.

This is Key! Obedience is better than sacrifice says the Lord (1 Samuel 15:22).

We cannot sacrifice our identity as a wife by doing things that single women do when their boyfriend is not treating them right. Okay! Wife, we should never degrade ourselves by doing disrespectful things behind our husband's back. Have self-control!

Now, let's get back to what is needed in order to have God in You. We know that we must possess God's fruit of the

Spirit. We know that we must put on the whole armor of God. We also recognize that we must pray day in and day out. Wife, what does it actually mean when we pray though? Get this! This is Key, When we pray, prayer is connecting us to the most high God in spirit. Once in connection with the Most High God, then our heart can be changed from a stony heart to a softened heart. Then our softened heart will begin to connect with the truths of God and what thus say the Lord. This is where God is truly in us. We always hear, "Pray about this," and, "Pray about that."

Why?

For one, the Bible tells us to **"pray without ceasing"** **(1 Thessalonians 5:17 KJV)**.

Secondly, it builds relationship with God due to the constant communication.

Third, prayer builds up our strength to deal with unfavorable circumstances.

Fourth, prayer stimulates the plans that God has for us and activates His will to release them.

So, after we have prayed, we must shift our focus. We no longer should focus on the hurt. Our focus should be on the healing. Wife, we should not dwell on and on about the disaster but look toward a new destination in marriage. When we pray, our problems have now been given to the Problem Solver. The only thing we have to do next is stand on the Lord's promises.

> ***For all the promises of God in him are <u>Yea</u>, and in him <u>Amen</u>, unto the glory of God by us.***
> **2 Corinthians 1:20 (KJV)**

The Lord's promises are found within the Word of God. It is imperative that we read God's Holy Word of the New Testament and the Old Testament within the Holy Bible. This is referred to as feeding God's spirit within us. Wife, when we feed our spiritual being, it becomes stronger, along with our desire to walk in love. We should meditate on God's Word and pray every word back to *Him* that pertains to our situation. Wife, we should remind God in prayer of what *He* said according to the Holy Bible. Furthermore, after we have prayed, we are now in position for a breakthrough. When a breakthrough happens, one may conclude that God must have heard our cries; we must have been found pleasing to God, and righteousness must have been our portion. **For the Bible declares in James 5:16 (KJV) that "the effectual fervent prayer of the righteous man availeth much."** So, if we are being righteous for God, then we are walking with God inside of us. The God in us has the power to change the way we look at the worst in our marriage. That same power has the authority to bind up the demonic spirits that have invaded our marriage so that the worst season can be changed for the better.

Verily I say unto you, Whatsoever ye shall bind on earth shall be bound in heaven: and whatsoever ye shall loose on earth shall be loosed in heaven. Matthew 18:18 (KJV)

AMEN!

THAT'S THE WORD!

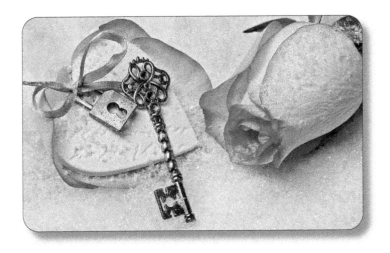

Chapter 3

Seasons

(For Better or for Worse)

With every season in life, there is change! We look forward to change when it comes to the four seasons of the year. We expect spring to bring April showers, so we carry our umbrella with us just in case. We expect fall to be a little chilly, so we make sure we wear our cute leather moto jacket outside. We know that winter is going to be extremely cold, so we make sure we buy a really warm coat with a matching hat to keep the heat inside our body. Then when summer comes, we make sure we are swimsuit ready since we know it is going to be super hot. Marriage can sometimes be like the seasons of the year—extremely cold or super hot. The thing about seasons in a marriage is that we are never prepared for the hot or cold temperatures like we are with the seasons of the year. It is just something that happens like a wave. One minute, we are hot and heavy in the sheets with our husband. Then, the next minute, we are cold as ice with an attitude about life's issues. Wow! Why do we let life's issues interfere with love? If we already know that life is not perfect, then we should know that our marriage is not going to be perfect or that our husband is not going to perfect everything, right? We made a vow to be with our husband for better or for worse. Why is that even a vow? This is Key! The Lord knew that there would come a time when marriage seemed the hardest and where marriage would not be in a blissful state. This is why marriage is for the Church. It is not for someone who does not believe in God. So, in honor of God and the covenant, we have to love our husband through the good times and love him even the more in the bad times. It is so easy to love when we are having the time of our lives, when all the bills are paid, and when our husband is spending quality time with us. The Lord knew that there would come a time when the better days seemed less than the bad days in our marriage. This is why it is so important to know the Word of God and abound in the Word of God so we can be prepared when the season changes. The Word of God tells us in **Ecclesiastes 3:1-8 (KJV)**:

> *To everything there is a season, and a time to every purpose under the heaven: A time to be born, and a time to die; a time to plant, and a time to pluck up that which is planted; A time to kill, and a time to heal; a time to break down, and a time to build up; A time to weep, and a time to laugh; a time to mourn, and a time to dance; A time to cast away stones, and a time*

to gather stones together; a time to embrace, and a time
to refrain from embracing; A time to get, and a time
to lose; a time to keep, and a time to cast away; A time
to rend, and a time to sew; a time to keep silence, and
a time to speak; A time to love, and a time to hate; a
time of war, and a time of peace.

The scripture never said, "A time to divorce." So, let's look at it. What could this scripture mean for marriage? The scripture says that there is a time to be born. For marriage, there is a time to birth something new, to birth change. Wife, we can birth a new perspective on dealing with the worst season in our marriage. In turn, that will birth a better season in our marriage. Right! We can change our bad attitude about the situation at hand. The scripture tells us that there is a time to die. Wife, we can die to ourselves and live for God. When we die to ourselves, we are simply denying our feelings of wants and needs and replacing them with God's love. God's love is merciful and full of grace. Wife, we get to show God's mercy and grace to our husband when we die to ourselves. In marriage, there is a time to plant. As mentioned in chapter one, when dirt has piled up on our marriage, our marriage is not dead and buried. It is planted for growth. So, we plant seeds when we endure difficulties in our marriage. We plant hope. We plant desires. We plant more love. Believe it or not, in storms, we are planting bonds with our husband that can never be broken. The scripture states that there is a time to kill. Wife, let's kill that negative thinking. Let us be optimistic about our marriage no matter what the condition or state it is in. God heals marriages, as the scripture declares that there is a time to heal. Wife, let's break down the communication barrier that is blocking understanding in our marriage for the time to break down in scripture. We breakdown the barrier by making sure our communication is clear and our words are comprehended correctly. Let us allow our husband to talk to us about anything, even if we do not want to hear it. We want to welcome our husband to converse about his day, his challenges, his interests, his ideas, his weaknesses, and his strengths. Then we want to build up our husband's character during the time to build up. Wife, we also should build up our confidence in the Lord by truly believing that the Lord will be a refuge in a time of trouble.

God is our refuge and strength, a very present help in trouble. Psalm 46:1 (KJV)

What is a refuge? According to Google English Dictionary, the definition of a refuge is something providing shelter. In other words, a refuge is a safe haven, a hiding place, security, and preservation. Wife, we have to believe that God will keep our marriage from going under in the time of trouble. This is not the time to gather stones but rather, a time to cast away stones. Pointing the finger at our husband is not the key. We all fall short, and we all sin. Some shortcomings lead to quiet storms, and other shortcomings lead to thunderstorms. Either way, we have to weather the storms in our marriage whether we are prepared or not. This is the time to embrace our marriage, as scripture tells us there is a time to embrace. *Wife, This is Key; we have to embrace all of the good that has ever happened in our marriage and use that energy to survive the worst.* We have to think about everything that God has blessed our marriage through and blessed our marriage with so that we will not lose sight of the promises of the Lord. Understanding is Key! There is a time to get an understanding. **The Bible tells us, "In all thy getting, get an understanding" (Proverbs 4:7 KJV).** Wife, we need to understand our husband's emotions. If not anything else, understanding the emotions behind conflicts in our marriage is vital to the survival of our marriage. Certain emotions tend to create distance, and other emotions tend to lead to non-verbal cues (facial expressions and body language.) Non-verbal cues can tell us a lot and can make or break our marriage when we ignore them or take heed of them. If we understand these emotions, we can consciously deal with them in a manner to dissect our husband's feelings and cater to his needs and the needs of our marriage.

Wife, there has never been a more fragile time than the season of war, as scripture states that there is a time of war. The war season is the most challenging season in a marriage. Without God, our marriage can be easily broken. Just think about the word "war." When hearing the word "war," we think about battle. We think of guns, ammunition, and bombs. We think of fighting and laying low. Wife, we know that in order to be at war, we have to be in warfare against something or somebody else. This is because we cannot war with our husband, right? Husband and wife are on the same team. So, who or what are we at war with? Wife, in those heated arguments, is Godly love being shown, or is the thought of God nowhere in mind? Wife, when frustration is at an all time high with your husband, is the spirit of meekness there? As mentioned in chapter 2, remember, *"For we wrestle not against flesh and blood, but against principalities, against powers, against the rulers of the darkness of this world, against spiritual wickedness in high places"* (**Ephesians 6:12 KJV**). Wife, This is Key! It is the spirit of wickedness and darkness that we are at war with within our marriage. The time for war is when the Enemy assaults our marriage. We have to put our war clothes on and strap up with the weapons of warfare. I am not talking about strapping up with a knife, a hammer, or a bat. I am not even talking about that black iron skillet. *"For the weapons of our warfare are not carnal, but mighty through God to the pulling down of strong holds"* (**2 Corinthians 10:4 KJV**). So, if we are thinking with a carnal (fleshly) mind, our mindset has to change to a spiritual mind so that we can bypass natural weapons of war and tap into "The Weapon of War." Well, what is the weapon? You ask. It is not *what*—it is WHO the weapon is. The weapon is Jesus! We have to declare that the devil is already defeated in JESUS's name. We have to plead the blood of Jesus over our situation, over our husband, and over our own life. In this war, we cannot give the devil any room to manipulate our mind to think that our husband is against us, in spite of the differences. Remember, we are chosen. So, when something arises in our marriage that is not equally understandable, it does not mean that we argue about it. It just means that there is a gray area that needs work. Arguments are the work of the devil. This is why arguments tend to get out of control. The wicked spirits never stop at a medium. They go as fast and far as we let them. The arguments tend to get bigger and bigger and bigger. As a result, somebody gets hurt, things get broken, we say hurtful things, and we hit below the belt. Then the next thing that comes out of the mouth of a devil: "*I Want a Divorce!*" Now, Satan thinks he is winning by creating division between a husband and a wife from a simple misunderstanding, from a mere disappointment, and from temporary financial difficulty.

When we find our marriage in this predicament, we have to get real serious with God. It is a very serious matter when our marriage is at stake. The Bible says pray in secret and the Lord will bless you openly (**Matthew 6:6**). Therefore, we have to create a secret territory to connect in the spirit with God. This secret territory is our war room! A war room is an area in your house that you use strictly for prayer. This is where we go to war in a spiritual connection with God. This area could be a closet, a utility room, the basement, or even a spare bedroom. The purpose of creating an area just for prayer is to focus on specific Bible scriptures written out on paper by you that pertain to each and every situation at hand and specific prayers that usher in the Spirit of God. When creating your war room, please remove all distractions in the area. We do not have time to waste drifting off in la-la land. Make sure the only things in sight are scriptures, prayers, and a Bible. If you want to get your heart and your mind ready for prayer while in your war room, just have your favorite gospel song playing in the background. If you do not have a favorite gospel song, here is one: "God Is Able" by Smokie Norful.

Now, how could the season of war be a season of blessings too? Good question! The answer is found in Jesus. When we seek Jesus for help, when we seek Jesus for understanding, when we seek Jesus for comfort, and when we cry out to God, our heart is at the very state that our God can use us for His glory. Our mind is humbled, and This is Key! Our eyes are on the Most High God. Now that is a blessing. Our mind could be lost without a clue as to whom to seek, where to get answers, and whom to breakdown in tears to without judgment. The great thing about crying out to God is that *He* turns our tears into internal joy, heartfelt joy, and unspeakable joy.

They that sow in tears shall reap in joy. Psalm 126:5 (KJV)
Amen!

Wife, when we first got married, that was a season of marital bliss, right? We had the honeymoon in the Caribbean, Honolulu, Punta Cana, Jamaica, or to a fancy hotel or motel, or Holiday Inn! Some of us just went home with rose petals, champagne, and cake. That was the bliss of marriage. Vacationing! In good health, money in the bank, smiling from ear to ear, for the better—this was us. Sickness, being broke, and facing the worst with our husband was the furthest from our mind and not even a thought. The reality has hit and the season of bliss has changed.

However, Wife, did we sign up for this?

I did not sign up for my husband to be sick; I need him to take care of me. I did not sign up for my husband to be broke; I need him to take care of me. I surely did not sign up for this awful and embarrassing situation. Is that how you think? I hope not! We sometimes fail to realize that we can be the one that get sick, lose our job, or get caught up in wrongdoing. I surely never thought that I would need my husband to wipe my behind. Yep, that happened! It was love. I was in so much pain while having a miscarriage. It was like all of my strength had been drained out of my body. I could not do anything for myself. My husband was right there at the hospital with me, and he held my hand. He helped me and catered to my every need. This is why we married. We married to have someone that will love us in the days and hours when we are at our lowest. *This is Key! The low season reveals true love.* There are many seasons in a marriage.

Seasons of love and happiness
Seasons of prosperity
Seasons of falling out of love
Seasons of unemployment
Seasons of grief & pain
Seasons of disappointment

Seasons of frustration
Seasons of highs & lows
Seasons of health and beauty
Seasons of falling back in love
Seasons of rejection
Seasons of embarrassment

Wife, let's talk about embarrassment. Has your husband ever embarrassed you in front of people? Or have you ever felt embarrassed by your husband's actions? Let me just say, you are not alone. Being embarrassed means you think highly of yourself and what happened did not resonate with the standards of your worth. Wife, our husbands are supposed to think highly of us. Our husbands' actions should align with our wife status. The status of being a wife is the most honorable, the most highly regarded and respectable fabric of a woman. So, when our husband's character display disregard for the esteem, admiration, and appreciation that we should receive from him, then embarrassment creeps in. When embarrassing situations happen, we are tormented in our mind with how other people may view us and the reflection it has on us as the wife of a husband that is misrepresenting us in the way he chooses to act. Embarrassing situations are triggered by neglect of some nature (i.e., the neglect of feelings, the neglect of morals, the neglect of love, the neglect of consideration, the neglect of commitment, neglect of family, or the neglect of worth). It is so easy to be embarrassed by our husband, especially when others can see what has happened or hear what happened. Our husband should be shame, not us, not thee Wife! Wife, we do not have to be ashamed, self-conscious, or even feel ridiculed by behaviors that are clearly dismissive toward our significance.

Here is why:

1. Did you create the situation? No!
2. Is the embarrassment because of your actions? No!
3. Your worth is not defined by someone else's treatment toward you.
4. Your value as a Wife is priceless.
5. Your worth and standards are measured by what you think of yourself.

How do I know? Honestly, I was so embarrassed by what my husband did that wrecked his own life. The humiliation and shame that I felt made me question the type of woman that I am. I felt that if I were a better woman, then my husband would not have chosen the road he trudged as my husband. Do you hear me? *As My Husband!* I beat myself up, back and forth, with questions. I asked myself, *Why would he do such a thing knowing that I am a spiritual person, knowing that I am an advocate for doing the right thing, knowing that he has a God-fearing wife. Why would he? Knowing that his wife is pregnant with a second child, and knowing he has a whole one year old son that needs him.* Then one day, I realized there was not anything wrong with my morals. There was not anything wrong with the way I encouraged him to do better. I realized that I

47

was still the queen despite his actions. I realized that, although my husband and I are one, I was not the one who had committed a crime. Are you kidding me! What a disaster! I did not make that dreadful mistake. I am actually still following the greatness of God and all that the Lord has for me. So, again, I questioned, *What am I embarrassed for? Oh, because it is my husband, and he is supposed to make me look good.* Right? Well, sometimes it is not about the look of a thing. It is not about how the disaster looks right now. Let me tell you, the situation my husband and I were in looked pretty bad, looked mighty catastrophic, and looked really rough. Oh, but God! When I looked to the hills from whence cometh my help, all of my help comes from the Lord (**Psalm 121 KJV**). I looked at the Master's hand of the thing because looks can be deceiving. The Master's hand showed me that it could be *worse*. The Master's hand showed me that we are blessed, in spite of calamity in our marriage. The hand of the Master showed me the purpose of the whole ordeal.

Before the disaster happened, my marriage was in shambles and pretty much over in my mind. My husband had been very negligent with his money and was blowing it on drugs. Our mortgage payments had fallen behind due to his addiction to drugs and my ignorance. Yes, my ignorance! I felt that I was not about to pay all of the bills by myself, even though I had the money to do so. How stupid of me to let my husband's burden create another burden when I could have prevented it. I wanted him to stop coming home high. He would say he was done popping pills, then within the next week, he was back at it again. I grew tired! My dream marriage had turned into a nightmare. I did not want our child witnessing his dad under the influence. It was the worst situation of my life. Just when I thought it couldn't get any worse, *it did!* The addiction turned into crime. The same week, my husband went to jail for the crime he committed. This was the same week I was scheduled to move out of our home, which he did not know. I was not moving out because we were behind on our mortgage. I was moving to prove the point that I was over the foolishness and that I was not about to continue to live under the same roof with a drug addict. He thought it was cool being high, but our marriage had fallen apart because of it. I told the Lord several times, "Lord, I lied, I cannot do 'for better or for worst' with him. This is too bad." My apartment was ready, and I was ready to be done stressing over the very things I had no control over. My husband left our home on a Monday evening and did not come home that night. I assumed that he was in the streets getting high and fell asleep somewhere. I didn't even call to see. Then, I received a call early Tuesday morning from him at the police station. He explained to me what happened and that he was going to be locked up for a very long time. His voice sounded so disheartened. I am sure he was crying. The phone call was pretty short, devastating, and very heart-wrenching.

After the call, something said in my spirit, *"You don't have to leave now!"* I ignored it! Then I moved to that apartment, with no dishwasher and no washer and dryer hook-up, anyway. Crazy! I rented our home out to a relative, gave away mostly all of our furniture, and got rid of all of his stuff. My spirit was so full of anger. I felt abandoned, unwanted, and unloved, even though I was the one leaving him before he got put behind bars.

Once my husband went to prison, God began to work on him and our marriage. At first, I was so unforgiving. My family and friends were saying, "Whelp, the marriage is over," and I thought so too. There was only one person, a good friend, which said to me, "Tiffany, you are still his wife; you have to be his wife." I heard her, however, I was not listening. But God! God started dealing with me on the basis of being a Christian and doing the right thing. The right thing was to forgive my husband. My husband asked me so many times to forgive him. I declined! He even brought to my remembrance of times that I had needed him the most. I said, "So!" I knew that I would have to forgive him one day though, simply because I needed peace in my mind. I could not rest holding on to his shortcomings. After I forgave him, a whole new journey of restoration began. That is when I realized it was God who said that I did not have to leave. If I had listened to God and not been so stubborn, I would have heard God saying, "*Be still, be quiet, sit down.*" Since then, my marriage has been restored, delivered, healed, and is thriving and growing purposefully. I moved back into our home, with my dishwasher and washer and dryer on deck. You hear me! So, it is not about how we look when going through a diabolical season. *It happens!*

Wife, the moral to the story is that we cannot be so angry in the "worst" season to the point where our ears are not unto God. **Anger stirs up wrath** (as mentioned in chapter 2)

(**Proverbs 15:1**). When anger stirs up the wrath, we end up doing unnecessary things and trying to fix the situation that is merely out of our control. *This is Key! We have to be in the right position with God to actually adhere to the voice of God.* I was out of position and focused on the wrong thing. My focus was on getting out of the worst season in my marriage. Instead, I should have been focused on the Most High God much, much sooner than this. So, Wife, do not wimp away when something seems embarrassing because it is not. It is life. It is a season that will pass.

The truth of the matter is that no marriage is perfect. Every marriage will have its shortcomings and challenges. The key factor in surviving is how we handle each season whether good or bad. If we handle the good seasons of marriage with respect, communication, love, stability, care, and with responsibility, then when the difficult seasons arise, we should keep that same loyalty as the wife and provide balance in the face of instability. There is no such thing as 50/50 in marriage. There probably will never be a 100/100 percent neither because of life's ups and downs. Wife, when our husband is unable to give 100 percent, then we provide the extra and pivot into the woman our husband needs. My husband needed me to pick up the slack, and I dropped the ball due to my ego and the standards I possess.

Wife, This is Key: Do not let your pride, your standards, or your big ego stop you from covering when your husband is down, whether he is down because of unemployment, irrespon-sibility, or addiction.

Remember, you are still THEE WIFE. When we find our-selves in a difficult season in marriage, it is important to recog-nize the source. What is the source? The source is the probable cause of difficulty. The difficulties in marriage run deep, from finances being too low to having to borrow money to make ends meet, to neglect, to cheating, to too much pride, to rejec-tion, to petty arguments, to communication deficiency. When we understand the culprit, we can begin to think rationally about ways to overcome the obstacles within our marriage.

The obstacles that I had to overcome hit me all at once. Embarrassment, rejection, and abandonment were all bun-dled into one situation with my husband. I was left to deal with the smoke, and it was pretty thick. I was supposed to be happy about being a new mom. On the contrary, I was sad about having to be a single mom that was married to an absent husband.

God the Almighty is the only one who kept me sustained. I was so depressed, felt so unhappy, and nobody knew it. Everybody seemed to think that I was so strong, so I pretended to be okay. Little did they know, as I pretended, I was on my knees praying. I was driving in my car, praying, I was at work in the bathroom, praying for strength, for help, and for my husband. It was the prayers that changed me, strengthened me, and gave me hope, which helped me build my faith back up in God.

Wife, This is Key! The same goes for you; it will be the prayers that make the difference and help in perseverance to overcome any situation in your marriage.

The Bible declares in Romans 5:3-5 (NIV)"Not only so, but we also glory in our sufferings, because we know that suffering produces perseverance; perseverance, character; and character, hope. And hope does not put us to shame, because God's love has been poured out into our hearts through the Holy Spirit, who has been given to us."

So, though we go through trials in our marriage, it is a push; it is a press toward God's love, God's protection, and God's purpose. Wife, when we need strength due to our marriage being at its worst, we will be able to see God at His best.

How?

Because the power of God is made perfect in our weakness and His power will rest upon us (2 Corinthians 12:9).

This is Key! At the end of the day, in order to keep the vow "For better or for worse" when the worst has embarrassed you, drained you, lied to you, exposed you, rejected you, disrespected you, or cheated you, you have to *forgive. Period!*

Chapter 4

True Forgiveness

(Restoring While Healing)

How do I forgive my husband when I cannot even believe he did such a thing to me—*to us?*

Wow! Wife, I know this feeling so well. The first step is to believe it, feel it, and address it within yourself. Admit to yourself any and every feeling that you have, even if you have to write it down and take a picture. It happened! Now, what can you change about it happening? *Nothing!* Nevertheless, something can be changed. What can be changed? You ask. Your heart! The heart of the matter can be changed. See, right now, in unforgiveness, everything is disgusting about your husband. Everything about the marriage is on the line. In unforgiveness, everything that ever happened good is thrown out the window. Harboring unforgiveness in your heart is ugly, and it stinks. It actually has a stank look. Really! A stank look! There are no smiles in unforgiveness and definitely no laughter. Unforgiveness is actually stressful. Whew! You are angry all the time. You're always in deep thought, repeating your thoughts over and over again. You're always experiencing the hurt day after day by constantly holding on to the offense. Unforgiveness is actually dangerous. You'll send your own self to hell walking around your house and to the mailbox holding on to unforgiveness. In fact, you will be more tempted to do the wrong things when carrying around an offense made by your husband. Wife, in unforgiveness, the devil takes your mind and has you thinking of all types of foolishness to get into because of the situation you just cannot believe. This is why it is so important to forgive. Our heart is at stake and even our own life.

Wife, first of all, do you even know what it actually means to forgive?

Let's look at it.

Forgiveness Is Love!

First and foremost, we know that we have to be forgiven by God Almighty in order to walk freely without guilt, shame, embarrassment, or bondage. The reason why God forgives us is because He loves us to no end. God's love is true forgiveness. When God forgives us, God forgets the offense; He forgets the sin committed against *His* Word. Then God restores us to the "perfect" being. There is no record of wrong kept with God. It is commanded of us to forgive as God the Almighty forgives us.

***And be ye kind one to another, tenderhearted,
forgiving one another, even as God for Christ's sake
hath forgiven you.* Ephesians 4:32 (KJV)**

I know that we are not even close to being just like God. Therefore, it is challenging for us to forgive when we have been wronged, hurt, or broken within our marriage, which is supposed to constantly feed love to us.

Wife, This is Key! Consider this:

1. Forgiving is being obedient to God.
2. Forgiving is setting yourself free from anger, bitterness, and retaliation.
3. Forgiving is a part of showing your love for your husband and our Father God in Heaven.
4. Forgiving is not saying the offense was and is acceptable.
5. Forgiving is saying that you value your inner spirit too much to hold on to a grudge that distorts your thinking, clogs up your mind, and adds uncontrollable stress that tear down your health.

A marriage built on love demands forgiveness. As stated in chapter 1, love hides a multitude of fault. This means that love wins over any situation, mishap, ordeal, sin, or circumstance. If the circumstance was infidelity, guess what? Love still wins. Wife, even though God has given us a release from our husband for adulterous sin, love covers adultery too. Wow! It is not stupid to stay, and it is definitely not ruthless to leave. Choose wisely! Just know that love conquers all things, and it does not stop even if you choose to leave. So, think about going through life still with a heart full of love for the man you left because of an affair that is forgivable. This is Key! Sin is sin, and lust is definitely one of the devil's mechanisms to separate husband and wife. Lust is so far away from love and works totally against love. This means that lust is against God because God is love. So, Wife, let adultery, lust, and the sinful nature of flesh be between God and the husband. This way, it removes the burden off of us and allows God to deal with our husband. Wife, when we understand the way God works, we can let God do the punishing and let God teach the lessons when our husband has sinned, stepped out, and/or committed adultery. This is not saying be *Ooh-Boo the Fool*. All we have to do is be the Wife and let God be God with *His* almighty, all-knowing, and all-powerful being. I do not condone cheating. I just know that cheating has torn a lot of families apart that could have been saved. As a matter of fact, I come against the spirit of infidelity. Wife, we cast down the desires of the wicked. We bind the force of adultery, right now, in the mighty name of Jesus. I command the enemy of division to flee. I declare and decree a forgiving heart and a forgiving mind, in Jesus's name. Amen!

Forgiveness Is Forgetting the Offense!

Hold on now! Wife! Forgiveness is about forgetting, just like God forgets our sins. I know that we, as humans, will not forget at all. That's funny! Literally, we will remember every detail, every word, every action, and every feeling of the offense. We will remember the day, the hour, and the exact year. Wow! Our mind is so full of memories, good and bad, the blessed and the mess. ***This is Key! Forgiveness is about putting your best thoughts over the mess thoughts.*** Read that sentence again! Wife, when we are trying to move on to a new day and get passed the dooms day, we have to switch our mind from the negatives of the situation to the positives of other things that are going on in our life. We have to overlook that bad thought really quick! As soon as negativity creeps in, *shut it down!* As soon as bad thoughts of the husband messing up the money overcomes you, *shut it down!* As soon as flashbacks of the husband acting a fool under the influence overtake your mind, *shut it down* with "That's the past." Yep, anything that is not of today is the past. Wife, if we keep bringing up past things, then we will never be able to operate in the present, the today! We can choose to encourage our husband to do the right thing today without bringing up old things or his short-comings of yesterday. As a matter of fact, Wife, we should forget about ever bringing up the offense again. If we have already discussed the matter with our husband, went to bed, woke up, and are going about a new day, then the issue is dead! So bury it! If you feel uneasy about the outcome of the discussion, the apology or lack of an apology, and want to say something else you thought of, take it up with God! Tell God! The Lord will be your helper and defense in resolving the matter wholeheartedly. If you hold on to unresolved matters in your mind, you will start imagining things and creating scenarios that do not even exist. Wife, then you will find yourself acting off of fear. Yes, fear! Fear is a mechanism of the devil that is planted in our mind when we hold on to an offense. This is when irrational behavior starts due to the fear of an offense happening again. Wife, our marriage will never get to the right place if we let fear in. As a matter of fact, fear drives out perfect love! This is Key! **"For God hath not given us the spirit of fear; but of power, and of love, and of a sound mind"** (2 Timothy 1:7 KJV). So, let us not operate in fear as the Enemy will have us to do in regard to our marriage. Do not be afraid to forget the offense, look past the offense, or dismiss the offense. For with God, all things are made possible if we just believe. So, how do we keep from bringing up the past when it's on the forefront of our brain? Good question! The answer is *breathe!* Don't talk, just listen! The Enemy wants us to live in the mess. You know the saying, "Can't cry over spilled milk." Crying is not going to put the milk back in the cup. It is done! Just clean it up. *This is Key! Wife, just clean it up! Clean your thoughts up with the Word of God. Amen!*

True Forgiveness Is Restoring

Brethren, if a man be overtaken in a fault, ye which are spiritual, RESTORE such an one in the spirit of meekness; considering thyself, lest thou also be tempted.
Galatians 6:1 (KJV)

Wife, true forgiveness is restoring the person at fault back to good graces as if there was no fault at all. Let's look at the word "restore." What does it really mean?

According to Google English Dictionary, *restore* means to …

❖ Bring back (a previous right, practice, custom, or situation); reinstate;

❖ Return (someone or something) to a former condition, place, or position; or

❖ Repair or renovate (a building, work of art, vehicle, etc.) so as to return it to its original condition.

Now that we know what it means to restore, Wife, why do you think restoration is required as a result of forgiveness? Hm! Think about it … Why does God restore us after we have sinned against *His* will? It is because God is showing us true forgiveness by washing our slate clean and giving us another chance to get it right without holding a grudge. Wife, This is Key; we have to restore our husband back to the same condition of friendship and love that he was in before the offense happened after we have forgiven him. Why? Think about it … What is so grand about forgiveness if the relationship is not restored as if nothing ever happened? Huh! Forgiveness is grand! Anything that God constructs is grand. *God created forgiveness so that we wouldn't be stuck in sin, stuck in wrongdoing, stuck in unhappiness, stuck going to Hell, stuck on the wrong side, stuck in mistakes, or stuck as the devil's advocate.* So, now we know that we do not have to condemn our husband for wrongdoing. Most often wrong doing does not include love. Actually, who on earth is thinking about love when the pleasures, gains, pockets, and addictions are on the forefront of our brain when faced with adversity? A husband should be! Huh?

Wife, you may be asking yourself, *How can I restore my husband when I am still hurt and healing is far from my mind?*

Good question! Once we forgive and relinquish all rights to be angry. We must swallow the pain, the disbelief, and the audacity, then we can begin healing with restoration. How so? Well, when we set the weight aside (cause it's a heavy weight) and make the decision to stay in spite of hurt and disappointment, the only way to healing is by letting go of what was done and letting God steer our emotions, guide our mind, and guard our heart. Speaking of guarding the heart, there is a misconception behind the meaning of "guarding the heart." Many people think that to guard our heart, we have to dismiss the person that has offended us. Wrong! Wife, we do not have to block our husband out of our heart and out of our life thinking that will safeguard us. Instead, and This is Key, we have to give our heart to God so that God can be our protector. Wife, when God is in charge of protecting our heart, there is nothing that one can do that can break our heart. Really! Let me tell you why. Wife, when our heart is in God's hand, God is always giving revelation to us. God is always speaking to our heart. There are no secrets that can be hidden from us. We can trust that the Lord will reveal to us foul play. God will soften our heart so much that we will have more compassion, more mercy, and more grace for our husband. Healing is in God's hands. So, if our heart is in God's hands, then healing is our portion as a result. Wife, go ahead and consciously restore your husband by embracing him like nothing ever happened. Resume being the loving, concerned, willful wife. When triggers outside of your control happen, try to neglect the negative emotions that may spur from natural thoughts. Wife, where there is shame, make the conscious decision to stand up, standby, and be a proud wife. Healing takes place in the motions of true forgiveness. Trust!

Chapter 5

Trusting (After the Let Down)

Trust in the Lord with all thine heart; and lean not unto thine own understanding. In all thy ways acknowledge him, and he shall direct thy paths. **Proverbs 3:5-6 (KJV)**

Wife! One thing is for sure, and two things are for certain: Trust is one of the most important elements of a great marriage, and without it, our marriage will surely fail. When trust is broken, it may seem like the marriage is over. It may seem like there is no way to trust our husband again. The devil will make it seem impossible to see past our husband letting us down. Wife, let me just tell you, there is a way to regain trust in our marriage, and it is not the way of the world—it is the way of God. This is Key! We have to put all of our *trust* in the Lord.

Wife, let's look at the meaning of trust. The Merriam-Webster Dictionary shows that *trust* means "**assured reliance on the character, ability, strength, or truth of someone or**

something: one in which confidence is placed: dependence on something future or contingent."

Wow! So, when we think about putting all of our trust in God, let us think about the character, ability, strength, and truth of Jesus that has been proven to do things seemingly impossible. There is no doubt about what Jesus is able to do because He has done miraculous things for people. Wife, I know that before we trust, we always have to see a track record that will let us know if we can trust a person. Well, the track record of Jesus is written in the Holy Bible. Listed below are a few miraculous things Jesus did, but I dare you to go read about it for yourself.

Jesus turned water into wine
(**John 2:1-11 KJV**).

Jesus drove out an evil/unclean spirit in a man
(**Mark 1:21-28 KJV**).

Jesus healed the woman with an issue of blood
(**Luke 8: 42- 48 KJV**).

Jesus made the blinded eyes see
(**Matthew 9:27- 31 KJV**).

Jesus fed 5,000 people with five loaves of bread and two fish
(**Matthew 14:13-21 KJV**).

Jesus calmed the storm on the sea with just a word
(**Matthew 8:23-27 KJV**).

Jesus walked on water
(**John 6:16-21 KJV**).

Jesus raised Lazarus from the dead
(**John 11:38- 44 KJV**).

If that is not enough to trust in God to do the impossible… What about Jesus raising from the dead Himself with All Power in His hands? Hold my mule, I'm going to shout right here!

See! All of these things were done for the belief of Jesus. God is saying that all we have to do is believe in the power and ability of Jesus to receive what God has for our life and our marriage.

Wife, This is Key! Believe that it is very possible to re-gain trust in our husband by trusting God first. Wife, we have to be intentional when we decide to renew trust. If we intend to build up our marriage, we cannot hold back the vital element that makes marriage great. Without trust, our marriage will diminish even the more. Trust is our safety net. We are safe when we can trust our husband. I know, after we have been let down, we feel that trust is long gone. In which, long gone is not too far gone. That means that the road back to trust will be trying. And that's okay! Marriage is trying every day. It is trying to fulfill our wifely duties, trying to fulfill our husband's needs, and trying to be fulfilled. This is Key! When we try, we will succeed in it, get better at it, or fail. Either way, trying will make all the difference. Wife, we need our husband to possess the qualities of being truthful, reliable, understanding, secure, and team-spirited. This is why we have to trust God to help us rebuild. We have to trust God to renew our heart. Wife, we even have to trust God to upgrade our husband with the necessary qualities needed. Trusting God will give us a sense of comfort in knowing that God never fails. So, even though trust has to be earned after it has been broken, rest assured that God will make a way somehow. In order to start trusting God fully, we have to throw every little piece of doubt in the trash. We should not let our actions be led by our own understanding because our understanding is carnal. Carnal understanding has no place with spiritual beliefs and bounds.

Wife, all we have to do is acknowledge God in all of our efforts. Acknowledging God means to consult with *Him* about everything. Let God be the first to know your thoughts, to know your wants, and to know your needs. Voice your concerns with God first so that whatever you are dealing with is before the Father. The Lord will then encourage us to be steady, to be fair, and to be wise in our marriage. Wife, I know that the choice to rebuild trust is frightening. As Joyce Meyers said, *"Do it afraid!"* (2018)

Question: How do we continue to trust God when God has not done for us what we "feel" needs to be done?

Wife, we then have to just trust God's plan and not let the unfulfillment of our own plans distract us. **Jeremiah 29:11 (KJV) says, *"For I know the thoughts that I think toward you, saith the Lord, thoughts of peace, and not of evil, to give you an expected end."*** This is Key! The Lord already knows how our marriage is going, what needs to be fixed, how trust was lost, what is needed to rebuild it, when the storm will be over, and if our husband will be receptive to change. The Lord knows! So, Wife, all we have left to do is activate and keep our faith in trusting what God already knows and trusting that *His* expected end is way better than what we expect and feel should be done. This is Key! God's expectation for marriage is that marriage be a ministry of love and happiness between two people, male and female, forever. Forever is Key!

Chapter 6

Love and Happiness

(To Stand the Test of Time)

For the vision is yet for an appointed time, but at the end it shall speak, and not lie: though it tarry, wait for it; because it will surely come, it will not tarry.
Habakkuk 2:3 (KJV)

Wife, one vision that I know we all have as a wife is for our marriage to last forever with love and happiness. It is really unfortunate that marriages in today's world are not lasting long. I know that we as women have grown to be "super-women" and have zero tolerance with a mindset of not needing a man for anything. So, I get it! We do not have to deal with a man's crap. Needless to say, marriage should bring about a difference in the way we handle things that pertain to the sincerity of our commitments. *Thinking of our husband as we think of our own self is Key when going through* *hardship.* Many people never stop to put the shoe on the other foot. The statistics say that most marriages end within the first five years. If you made it past the five-year mark, congrats to you, and still, there may be work to do. Wife, in order to stand the test of time while in the worst season of marriage, a strong foundation is Key. Being equally yoked is also a major factor in the long haul when trials are invading our marriage. Remembering the purpose of getting married will also keep us from breaking our covenant.

The foundation of a marriage is the most important element with which our marriage can and will be supported through the worst. First and foremost, a strong foundation is built upon a number of things that include respect. However, let's touch base on one of the greatest aspects of a marital foundation that will help bridge the gap when marriage seems to be struggling. This is Key—*Intimacy!* Wife, intimacy is a major Key in a marriage built to last. Intimacy is the friendship that connects us to our husband. Intimacy is the closeness that allows us to feel comfortable with being our self around our husband. Intimacy is the openness to express our heart, our mind, and our feelings. Intimacy requires a great deal of vulnerability. Wife, you should know that vulnerability happens when we unleash hurt, release forgiveness, and trust. Trust is actually the main ingredient of intimacy. So, how do we embrace intimacy while rebuilding trust? The short answer is: God! The long answer includes a story of my life. I mentioned in chapter four that my marriage was in shambles before my husband went to prison. There was a total disconnect between us because of the lack of intimacy during the worst season of our marriage. There was no real communication present; there were no eye-to-eye conversations. We did not have any "Netflix and chill" nights. We stopped having lunch and dinner together. There was no breakfast in bed going on. We surely did not do any physical touching. I could not even tell you the last time we had held hands. There was no intimacy outside of our bedroom, which played a major part in the destruction of our marriage.

After my husband was sentenced to serve one hundred and eleven months in prison, the real work in my marriage began. God was dealing with me so heavily; I had no choice but to do the work. How could I claim to be a Christian, a child of God, and not be there for my husband, even though the situation was worse than I ever imagined? So, no, I had no choice! I kept hearing God say, "Embrace your marriage," "Embrace your marriage," *"Embrace Your Marriage!"* What did that mean for me? My husband was way across county locked up, and I was in our home with our children by myself. This was a hard situation to swallow and embrace. As I continued to seek God, God continued to rest His love upon my husband and me. My husband started reading the Word of God again. Then we started reading the Word of God together. Yes, together! We would tell each other the book to read in the Bible. Then we would send each other messages about what we read and our perspectives of it. God surely was moving through email messages, phone calls, and letters. Our physical visits became more intimate. We had eye-to-eye communication. We had mental stimulation. Our excitement for each other had resurfaced. We were able to talk about our deepest feelings without judgment. We were more open about our own outlook on the disruptions in our marriage. We now have understanding in places where there was misunderstanding. We fell in love all over again. It was spirit to spirit and heart to heart. *This is Key! A marriage built on spiritual intimacy has a foundation that is rock-solid. Spiritual intimacy can never be broken.* That bond will always be there in the better seasons to make things sweeter and during the worst seasons to resurrect and rebuild the dead things in our marriage. Wife, this is why it is so important for us to be equally yoked with our husband.

Being Equally Yoked

Being equally yoked means believing in the same God, following the same religion, sharing the same spiritual guidance, having the same mission in marriage, and believing in the same purpose for marriage. When two people are tied together, it is important for the two to be on one accord, moving in the same direction.

The Bible questions, "How can two walk together unless they are in agreement with one another?" (Amos 3:3 KJV).

Being equally yoked is an advantage in marriage. When tough trials happen, we are then able to come together with our husband on a level that is already understood. Wife, it is understood that prayer will fix it. Wife, it will be understood that patience is a virtue. Wife, our husband will appreciate and understand the reasoning behind standing in the gap spiritually. Our husband will also know the importance of not letting the worst seasons deter the whole marriage from its purpose.

Being equally yoked will also determine the structure of our marriage. The structure is what builds the marriage and the bond. Praying together builds structure. Fasting together builds structure. Going to church together builds structure. Ministering to each other builds structure too. Wife, these things are done without a hassle when we are equally yoked with our husband.

How can one become equally yoked with an unsaved husband?

This is Key! Wife, are you saved? (Back to the very first question that was asked at the very beginning of this book.) The Bible reveals that a sanctified wife sanctifies her husband.

For the unbelieving husband is sanctified by the wife, and the unbelieving wife is sanctified by the husband.
1 Corinthians 7:14 (KJV)

Really! Sanctified? What does it mean to be sanctified? Wife, in order to be sanctified, you must first be saved. Then when you separate yourself from worldly things, worldly influences, and worldly people, and maintain your life with Godly things, Godly influence, and Godly people, you become sanctified. Becoming sanctified is a way of life. It is how we act, how we respond to things, what we do on the regular, and how we treat our husband in spite of the circumstances. When our husband is a constant witness to our Godly behavior and Godly aura, it then rubs off on him. Soon, he will be like, "I *wanna* be down," because of the Holy Spirit working to save our husband on our behalf. Once our husband is on board spiritually, the disconnect will start connecting in the areas that our marriage is suffering in. Those connections will start to plant seeds in places where there was only dirt. More love will start to blossom, more faith in our marriage surviving will be in our heart, there will be more laughter in situations that are out of our control, and there will be more happiness within. The foundation of our marriage will begin to solidify into rock-solid brick that is not easily broken. ***This is Key! The purpose of our marriage will be able to manifest.*** Amen!

Remembering the Purpose

Wife, we would like to think that marriage is all about love and happiness when in reality, marriage is all about fulfilling God's given purpose for marriage. God's given purpose for marriage is for man and wife to be fruitful together, for man and wife to be helpers to one another, and for man and wife to create a family that prays and stays together.

The Bible confirms that what God has joined together, let no man put asunder (Matthew 19:6 KJV).

Wife, that is including you! Some of us did not get married with God's purpose in mind, but we did, however, have our own purpose for marrying. This is Key! It is vital to keep our own purpose for our marriage alive. When faced with hard trials in marriage, we have to remember the *why* underneath the *why*. When we do that, we are able to buckle up and embrace our marriage with a mindset to push through.

What is your purpose for getting married?

Is it to be a power couple? Why?

Is it to break generational curses? Why?

Is it to overcome broken homes? Why?

Is it to change family dynamics? Why?

Is it to fulfill the American dream? Why?

Is it to show reverence for God with your body? Why?

Wife, one of the main purposes for me getting married was to honor God with my body. As I mentioned in Chapter 1, The Bible asserts that "it is better to marry than to burn" in the fire if you just can't stop yourself from being physically intimate with someone (1 Corinthians 7:9). I had always wanted the physical intimacy that my man and I shared to be "right" in the eyes of the Lord. I was so sick of asking the Lord for forgiveness for that one thing over and over again. Clearly, I liked getting physical. Wife, let us be honest. We all do! I struggled for so long thinking that getting physical with my man equated to love. In the holy reality, it equates to sin if the man is not your husband. This is Key! Marriage equates to love. At least, it's supposed to. Being married helped me a whole lot in living a saved life. It saved me from a life of fornication. *This is Key! Jesus is the only one that saves.* Because I thought that my marriage saved me from fornication, I was faced with being married to a physically absent husband. Now what? Since my husband had been locked up, the devil played and preyed on me. My thoughts were consumed with everything about sex. Although the devil had not anything to do with my hormones, Lucifer had a lot to do with my thinking. Listening to secular music made my thoughts even worse. I was in temptation, and my flesh yearned for flesh physically. At one point, I felt like I had no choice but to give in to my fleshly desires. However, I did have a choice. And Wife! This is Key! We have a choice to choose God. I had the choice to cast my fleshly desires on the Lord. I had the choice to pray more. I had the choice to feed my spirit more so that my flesh wouldn't over take me. It was not an easy journey, going without physical intimacy of which I craved. As a matter of fact, at one point, I thought it was hard. **The Bible says that the ways of a transgressor is hard (Proverbs 13:15 KJV).** What does that mean? It means that a sinner's life is difficult because they are doing everything in their own power and not with the power of the Lord. Because I knew that scripture down in my spirit, I knew that choosing God and following *His* commandments would make all the difference. I knew that I could depend on God's power to help me get through the lack of physical intimacy. I also had to remember that I sin against my own body if I lay down with a man that is not my husband. I cannot say that I did not fall short of the glory of God when I was not *seeking* God. What I can say is that my belief in the Lord and *His* Holy Word, which lined up with my purpose for marrying my husband, did not let me continue due to the feeling of guilt, defeat, and unworthiness. I felt like I was out of my character as a wife, as a Christian, and as a God-fearing woman. I was convicted! I fell down, but the Lord pulled me out of the pit and confirmed that I am better than that!

There is therefore now no condemnation to them which are in Christ Jesus, who walk not after the flesh, but after the Spirit. **Romans 8:1 (KJV)**

The Lord said, "*You are a wife!*" The Lord said that I did not have to lean on pleasure to cover the pain. Ultimately, I had to start denying myself of those fleshly desires. I had to stop entertaining conversations that could lead to sin. I had to stand on the Word of God. All I needed was a little more Jesus to help me keep the purpose for marrying my husband alive. *This is Key! When we remember our purposes for getting married, we are able to hold on a little while longer while the worst season is happening.* Nobody is perfect, but what is important is that we continue our marriage in love of what we started and stand the test of time.

Standing the Test of Time

Wife! Sometimes we have to make some tough decisions in order to endure through hard times. First, the most important, yet challenging, decision we have to make is to not waiver in the decision to stay through it all. There will be times and moments that will question this decision. In those times and moments, we have to push through. Push through by thinking of the reasons why you are staying. Secondly, we have to make the decision to dismiss those people (that may even be good people) that are against your decision to stay and that are compromising your position as a wife. Third, we have to make the decision to *wait!*

Wait to indulge in marital bliss again.

Wait on Jesus to change our husband's heart, mind, and ways.

Wait to feel that "in love" feeling again. (And believe me, it is possible!)

Most importantly, wait on the Lord to bless our marriage.

> ***But they that wait upon the Lord*** *shall renew their strength;*
> *they shall mount up with wings as eagles; they shall run, and*
> *not be weary; and they shall walk, and not faint.*
> **Isaiah 40:31 (KJV)**

Wife, waiting on the Lord to show up and show out in the worst season of marriage requires you to be still, but you will not be doing "nothing." There is a difference between being still and doing nothing! When you are being still, you are actually doing so much. You are allowing God to have *His* way with your husband and to have *His* way with you. Wife, you are not letting the devil win. You are *embracing the fruit of the Spirit — patience*—even in the chaos. Wife, when you begin to give God more attention than you are giving the problem in your marriage, the Lord will do a new thing in you. Everything is out of your hands and in the hands of the Potter, the Lord. Wife, your mindset will start changing to the mindset of Jesus. Jesus will start giving you revelation and visions of a successful marriage. This will motivate you in enduring through the worst.

Nevertheless, a strong marriage takes time to build. Wife, we know that time waits for no man. It ticks like a bomb! Do not panic. Marriage is not a sprint; it is a marathon. We hold the key to our destiny. In marriage, time is a key factor in creating what we all would like to have, and that's a good, successful marriage. If we treat our marriage like we are maintaining a brand-new house, our marriage will last forever. How so? The requirements to maintain a home are much like the requirements to maintain our marriage. ***This is Key! We have to make our marriage our home.*** A house is not a home if there is no love inside. The same goes for marriage. When something isn't working properly or breaks down inside the house, we have to fix it. We don't just throw the whole house away due to something that can be fixed. The same goes for marriage. It can be fixed!

Maintenance is Key! According to the Dictionary of International Trade, "maintenance" is described as "the work of keeping something in proper condition, care, or upkeep including: taking steps to avoid something breaking down or bringing something back to working order."

My definition of maintenance for marriage is described as the necessary emotional impartation of both spouses. Then the question becomes: What builds emotions? Wife, emotions are created by spending the necessary time and giving the necessary attention that captures one's soul. It's the heart-to-heart connections. It is being naked in front of each other in body, mind, and spirit. It is being open to correction. It is giving grace to one another. It's the laughter being shared. It is the *work* being done to alleviate the problems. So, maintenance could be as simple as having date nights on the regular. Maintenance could also be therapy with a marriage counselor to help break the ice. Maintenance could very well mean alcohol or drug rehab for your spouse. Maintenance could be consulting a money management coach. Seeing a therapist together for intimacy in the bedroom is a form of maintenance too. Maintenance includes all of *thee* above and whatever kind of **works** that are needed to be done in your marriage in order to stand the test of time.

Overall, Wife, we did not get married for show, and we definitely did not get married to get a divorce. I wrote this book to tell you that there is a rainbow at the end of the storm—God's promise rainbow that reminds us of His covenant with us! This is Key! You just have to keep hope alive, even through the darkest hour. Press through in your mind with hopeful thinking, looking on the bright side of things, letting the past be the past, letting what has been done be done, and giving no room to relive the moments of destruction. Wife, you should be praising God that the destruction did not destroy the marriage but put the marriage on a road to recovery, a road to replenishment, and a road less driven in today's world, and that's a road with God. I have shared with you many ways to endure through the worst seasons of marriage. The ways that I have shared, I can attest to them. I pray that you take heed and follow God. Your steps will be ordered in every situation that your marriage may come across. There is mercy on the Lord's side. We are standing in mercy every day. The mercy of the Lord will help us prevail in our marriage. Mercy will get us to the mark—the mark of salvation, the mark of peace, the mark of plenty, and the mark of living our best life with the man of our dreams, our husband!

This is Key! Be the Wife! Do your part! Stand your ground!

References

Scripture Quotations taken from the Holy Bible, New International Version, (NIV) Copyright 1973, 1978, 1984, 2011 by Biblica, Inc. Used by permission. All rights reserved.

Scripture Quotations taken from the New King James Version, (NKJV) Copyright 1982 by Thomas Nelson. Used by permission. All rights reserved.

Scripture Quotations taken from King James Version (KJV) – Public Domain

Maintenance. (2023). In *Dictionary of International Trade*. Retrieved from https://www.globalnegotiator.com

Refuge. (2023). Retrieved from *Google English Dictionary*. Oxford Languages

Restore. (2023). Retrieved from *Google English Dictionary*. Oxford Languages

Trust. (2023). In *Merriam-Webster Dictionary*. Retrieved from https://www.merriam-webster.com/dictionary/trust

Printed in the USA
CPSIA information can be obtained
at www.ICGtesting.com
LVHW071228270224
772868LV00015B/289